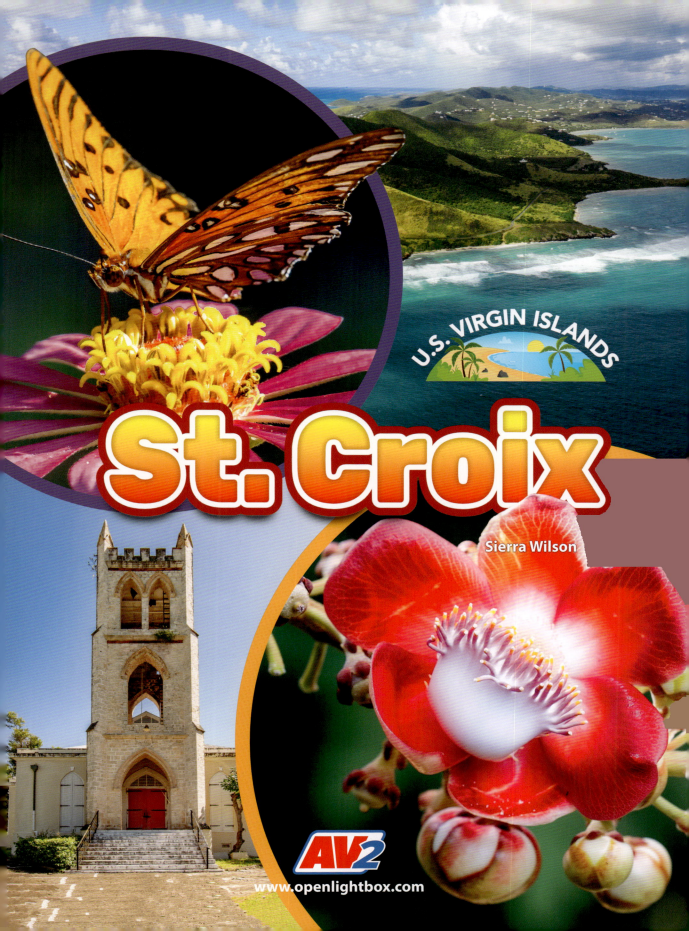

Step 1
Go to www.openlightbox.com

Step 2
Enter this unique code

VCQUNQEYD

Step 3
Explore your interactive eBook!

AV2 is optimized for use on any device

Your interactive eBook comes with...

Contents
Browse a live contents page to easily navigate through resources

Audio
Listen to sections of the book read aloud

Videos
Watch informative video clips

Weblinks
Gain additional information for research

Slideshows
View images and captions

Try This!
Complete activities and hands-on experiments

Key Words
Study vocabulary, and complete a matching word activity

Quizzes
Test your knowledge

Share
Share titles within your Learning Management System (LMS) or Library Circulation System

Citation
Create bibliographical references following APA, CMOS, and MLA styles

This title is part of our AV2 digital subscription

1-Year Grades K–5 Subscription
ISBN 978-1-7911-3320-7

Access hundreds of AV2 titles with our digital subscription.
Sign up for a FREE trial at www.openlightbox.com/trial

The digital components of this book are guaranteed to stay active for at least five years from the date of publication.

U.S. VIRGIN ISLANDS
St. Croix

CONTENTS
- 2   Interactive eBook Code
- 4   Welcome to St. Croix
- 6   Beginnings
- 8   The Island Today
- 10 Exploring St. Croix
- 12 Land and Climate
- 14 Plants and Animals
- 16 Places to See
- 18 Things to Do
- 20 Looking to the Future
- 22 Quiz Yourself on St. Croix
- 23 Key Words/Index

WELCOME TO
St. Croix

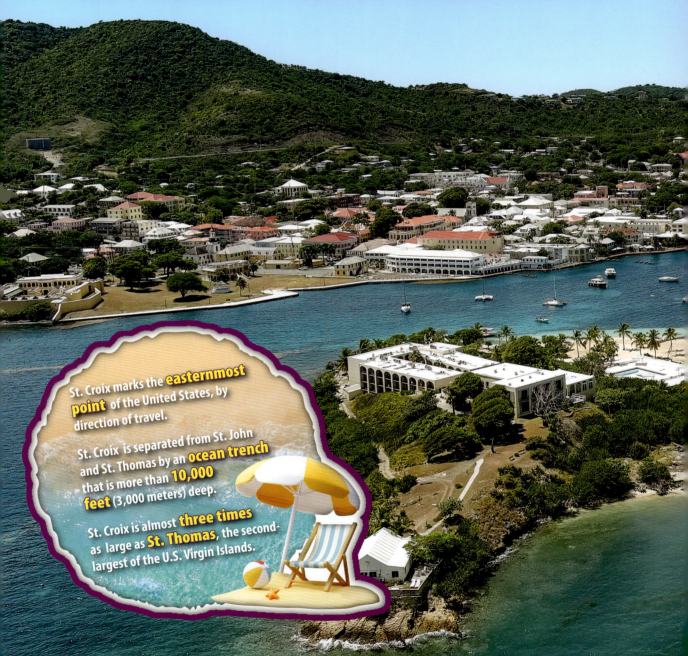

St. Croix marks the **easternmost point** of the United States, by direction of travel.

St. Croix is separated from St. John and St. Thomas by an **ocean trench** that is more than **10,000 feet** (3,000 meters) deep.

St. Croix is almost **three times** as large as **St. Thomas**, the second-largest of the U.S. Virgin Islands.

4 U.S. Virgin Islands

The northeastern part of the Caribbean Sea is home to an **archipelago** of about 50 islands. Known as the U.S. Virgin Islands, they have been a **territory** of the United States since 1917. There are three principal islands in the archipelago. These are St. Croix, St. Thomas, and St. John.

St. Croix is the largest of the U.S. Virgin Islands. Known as a beautiful, relaxing tourist destination, it has white-sand beaches, coral reefs, and green hills. It also has a variety of historic sites. St. Croix is known for its lively festivals and tasty restaurants. Cruise ships and tourist groups often visit the island.

Beginnings

St. Croix is part of an ancient undersea mountain range that includes many of the islands of the Caribbean Sea. The rocks that make up St. Croix are more than 80 million years old. They formed in the Cretaceous Period, when dinosaurs walked on Earth.

Christopher Columbus made four voyages to the New World between 1492 and 1504. He visited St. Croix on his second trip.

People first arrived in St. Croix about 2,500 years ago. These first inhabitants came from South America. Various **Indigenous** groups lived on St. Croix at different times. The Arawaks and the Caribs are two of the best known.

In 1493, Christopher Columbus visited St. Croix. He claimed it for Spain, but it was years before the Spanish began building settlements there. In 1625, English and Dutch settlers both came to St. Croix. For the next hundred years, European nations fought to control the island. St. Croix was seen as a valuable place to grow sugarcane for sugar. Tobacco and cotton were also grown there. People from Africa were enslaved and brought to the island to work on **plantations**. They were freed from slavery only in 1848. The United States bought St. Croix from Denmark in 1917.

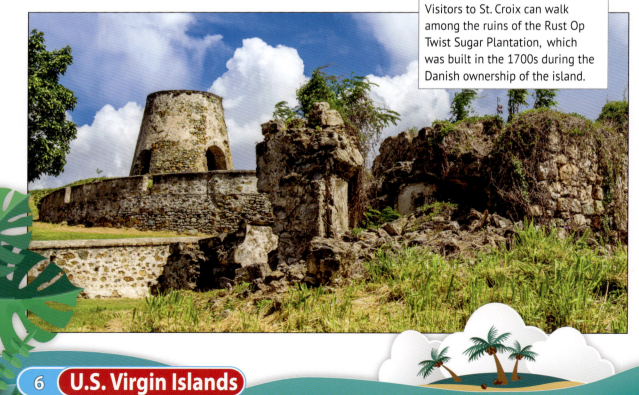

Visitors to St. Croix can walk among the ruins of the Rust Op Twist Sugar Plantation, which was built in the 1700s during the Danish ownership of the island.

6 U.S. Virgin Islands

St. Croix Timeline

2,500 years ago
Humans begin to live on St. Croix.

1493
Christopher Columbus briefly visits St. Croix while exploring the area.

1625
English and Dutch settlers come to St. Croix and fight for power.

1733
Denmark takes control of St. Croix and divides the island into plantations.

1848
Slavery is abolished in St. Croix.

1917
The United States purchases St. Croix for $25 million.

1927
Residents of St. Croix officially become U.S. citizens.

2025
The Caribbean Travel Awards names St. Croix the Caribbean Culinary Destination of the Year for the wide range of dining experiences offered on the island.

The Island Today

More than 40,000 people currently call St. Croix home. Known as Crucians, the island's residents mostly come from African **ancestry**. Other Crucians have European, Asian, and Latino ancestry. English is the most-spoken language on St. Croix. People also speak various **Creole** languages, along with Spanish and French. The main Creole language on St. Croix is called Crucian. It is a mixture of African, English, Portuguese, French, and Dutch languages.

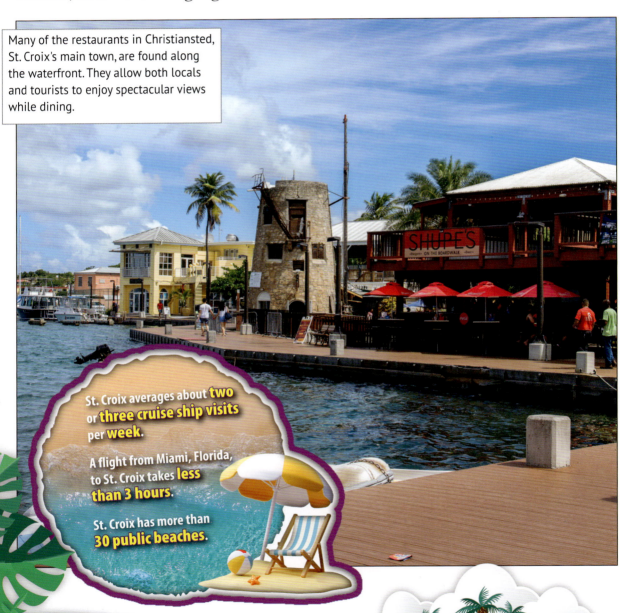

Many of the restaurants in Christiansted, St. Croix's main town, are found along the waterfront. They allow both locals and tourists to enjoy spectacular views while dining.

St. Croix averages about **two or three cruise ship visits per week.**

A flight from Miami, Florida, to St. Croix takes **less than 3 hours.**

St. Croix has more than **30 public beaches.**

U.S. Virgin Islands

Tourism is the largest industry in St. Croix. At least 100,000 tourists visit the island each year. Most arrive on cruise ships. St. Croix has a variety of resorts, restaurants, and tourist attractions to keep guests entertained. Agriculture is another part of St. Croix's economy. The island **exports** food and rum. It also makes and exports wristwatches.

For many years, St. Croix produced oil. The island's **oil refinery** was one of the largest in the world, producing about 500,000 barrels per day. Currently, the refinery is closed. This is due to concerns about its impact on the health of island residents. Dangerous chemicals are being cleaned from the refinery so that it can potentially reopen in the future.

St. Croix's farmers often sell their goods at local markets on the island.

St. Croix 9

Exploring St. Croix

St. Croix covers an area of about 84 square miles (218 square kilometers). It is located 65 miles (105 km) southeast of Puerto Rico and about 1,100 miles (1,770 km) from Florida. Even though St. Croix is the largest of the U.S. Virgin Islands, it is still quite small, measuring only 28 miles (45 km) long and 7 miles (11 km) wide.

Christiansted

Christiansted is the largest town on St. Croix, with a population of about 1,800. It was once the capital of the Danish West Indies. Many of its historical sites focus on this time period.

Frederiksted

Frederiksted is the second-largest community on St. Croix. Approximately 525 people live in and around the town. Frederiksted is known for its beautiful **architecture** and interesting historic sites. The town was also once a major site for **trade**.

10 U.S. Virgin Islands

Mount Eagle

Mount Eagle is the highest point on St. Croix. It reaches a height of about 1,165 feet (355 m). People can hike to the top of Mount Eagle for a wide view of the island.

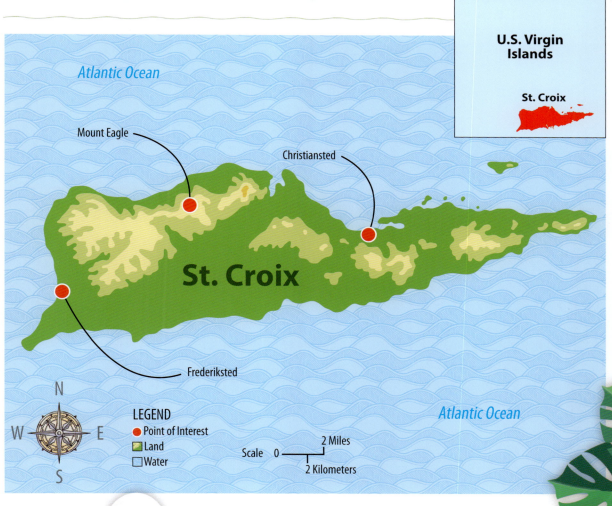

Land and Climate

St. Croix has many different **geographic** zones and features. The eastern side of the island is dry and rocky. It features grassy hills and cacti. The western side of the island is much wetter and greener. Fruit trees and ferns can be found growing on the mountainsides. The central part of the island has open, rolling fields.

The island's coastline features several bays and natural harbors. Tide pools can be found along the coast as well. A variety of sea creatures and plants can often been seen in these shallow pockets of seawater.

Point Udall is the easternmost point of St. Croix and the United States. The site is marked by a sundial called the Millennium Monument.

12 U.S. Virgin Islands

A number of small **cays** can be found off St. Croix's coast. The best-known is Protestant Cay. It is located near Christiansted. People enjoy taking a ferry to this cay and spending time on its white, sandy beaches.

St. Croix has a tropical climate. It is warm and sunny all year. **Trade winds** from the east blow across the area. These winds help to lower the **humidity** of the island. St. Croix gets about 50 inches (127 centimeters) of rain per year. Rainstorms usually only last a few minutes at a time.

Average High Temperatures

JAN	82°F (28°C)
FEB	82°F (28°C)
MAR	82°F (28°C)
APR	82°F (28°C)
MAY	84°F (29°C)
JUN	86°F (30°C)
JUL	86°F (30°C)
AUG	86°F (30°C)
SEP	86°F (30°C)
OCT	86°F (30°C)
NOV	84°F (29°C)
DEC	82°F (28°C)

Protestant Cay makes the most of the 4 acres (1.6 hectares) it covers. Besides its beaches, the island has a hotel and restaurant.

St. Croix 13

Plants and Animals

Many different types of plants and animals can be found on St. Croix. These include both tropical and **arid** plants. There are **mammals**, birds, **reptiles**, fish, and other types of animals. Some of the wildlife on St. Croix is **endemic**. Other wildlife, such as deer and mongooses, were brought by people.

St. Croix Agave

St. Croix agave is a **succulent** plant that is endemic to St. Croix. Also known as Eggers' agave, the plant can grow to be more than 5 feet (1.5 m) tall and send out a spike that can reach up to 20 feet (6.1 m) high. The blooms on this spike can be yellow or orange.

St. Croix Anole

The St. Croix anole is found only on St. Croix. It is an arboreal lizard, which means it resides mainly in trees. These small lizards can range in color from green to brown and often have orange or yellow **dewlaps**. They can be up to 2.5 inches (6.4 cm) in length, not including their tail.

14 U.S. Virgin Islands

Caribbean Hermit Crab

The Caribbean hermit crab is common throughout the region. It is typically found along coasts and in coastal forests. Caribbean hermit crabs can measure up to 6 inches (15 cm) in length. They feed on the remains of plants and other animals.

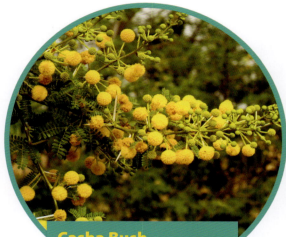

Casha Bush

The casha bush is one of St. Croix's most common trees and can be found throughout the island. The tree is known for its round, yellow blooms and its prickly thorns. It can grow to a height of about 26 feet (8.5 m).

Antillean Crested Hummingbird

The Antillean crested hummingbird can be seen throughout the eastern Caribbean. It is the smallest hummingbird in the region, measuring about 3.5 inches (9 cm) from head to tail. This hummingbird can be found in parks, gardens, and near forested areas. It is one of only a few hummingbirds to have a crest on the top of its head.

Places to See

St. Croix offers guests a variety of sites to visit. One of the most colorful is the St. George Village Botanical Garden. Located on the grounds of a former sugar plantation, it covers an area of more than 16 acres (6.5 ha) and is home to more than 1,000 different species of tropical plants.

Another popular destination is the Christiansted National Historic Site, which tells the story of the Danish **colonization** of the island. The site includes many different historic buildings. One is an old Danish fort called Fort Christiansvaern. It is well-preserved and considered a great place to connect with history.

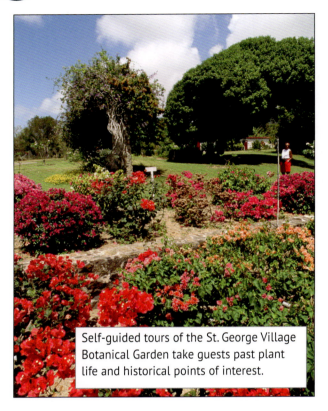

Self-guided tours of the St. George Village Botanical Garden take guests past plant life and historical points of interest.

Throughout its history, Fort Christiansvaern not only served as a military installation but also a prison, courthouse, and religious meeting place.

Taking part in festivals is also popular with tourists. For more than 25 years, St. Croix has hosted a food festival called the Taste of St. Croix every April. Thousands of people show up to sample unique dishes from local chefs, farms, and restaurants.

Another major event on the island is the Crucian Christmas Festival. This celebration offers a Caribbean slant to the festive season. It includes concerts, pageants, parades, food booths, and local arts, giving visitors the opportunity to experience the local culture of St. Croix.

Food booths are a popular fixture at most of the festivals held on St. Croix.

Local talent is often on display during the Crucian Christmas Festival.

The traditions connected with the **Crucian Christmas Festival** date back to the **1800s**.

Construction on **Fort Christiansvaern** began in **1738**.

From **100** to **900 AD**, the site of the St. George Village Botanical Garden was an Arawak village.

St. Croix 17

Things to Do

Only a limited number of visitors are allowed to tour Buck Island Reef National Park's underwater trail each day.

St. Croix's warm weather makes it an ideal place to enjoy outdoor activities. One of the most popular pastimes is visiting Buck Island Reef National Monument. Located off St. Croix's north coast, Buck Island is a protected area with several nature trails and beaches to explore. It also has a 4,554-acre (1,843-ha) coral reef. Divers and snorkelers can see hundreds of different fish species in the reef. There is even an underwater trail with informational plaques about marine life.

St. Croix offers tourists other diving and snorkeling opportunities as well. Night diving is popular off the pier in Frederiksted. With flashlights in hand, divers swim around and under the pier, trying to spot life in the water. They are often able to see octopuses, starfish, sea turtles, seahorses, and other sea creatures.

The Frederiksted pier extends more than 1,500 feet (457 m) from the town itself. It was built specifically as a cruise ship dock.

Swimming and relaxing on the beach are also popular activities in St. Croix. One notable spot is Rainbow Beach, near Frederiksted. It is known for its clear, calm waters and spectacular sunsets.

Another way to enjoy the waters of St. Croix is through boating. Tourists can go on group or private sailing tours. Some of these tours allow tourists to sail the boat. Many visitors choose to go kayaking. They often rent glass-bottomed kayaks and head over to the Salt River Bay National Historical Park and Ecological Preserve. The waters here are full of **bioluminescent** creatures.

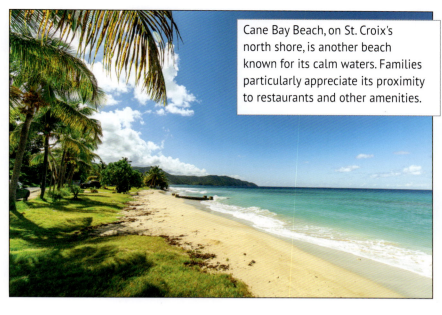

Cane Bay Beach, on St. Croix's north shore, is another beach known for its calm waters. Families particularly appreciate its proximity to restaurants and other amenities.

Visitors to St. Croix can personalize their trip by renting a catamaran. Having the boat to themselves allows tourists to plan their own itinerary and activities.

St. Croix 19

Looking to the Future

With all the water that surrounds St. Croix, it is difficult to imagine that it can be in short supply on the island. This is the case, however. The salt water of the sea cannot be used as drinking water, and the island has no lakes or rivers to provide the fresh water its residents need. Underground water sources are limited as well. Collecting rainwater can help, but St. Croix does not receive enough rain to make this a year-round solution. In fact, the island often experiences drought periods where very little rain falls at all. In the past, residents have been forced to purchase their water from private companies at great expense.

St. Croix homeowners opting to have water delivered may spend upwards of $100 for every 1,000 gallons (3,785 liters).

St. Croix's desalination plants use a process called reverse osmosis to remove salt from water. The process involves pushing water under high pressure through thin membranes to filter out the salt.

PROBLEM SOLVER

What do you think about the idea of turning salt water into fresh water? What might be some challenges of this process? What are the advantages and disadvantages?

To help supply St. Croix's residents with clean drinking water, the island has relied on saltwater **desalination** plants. These plants are able to turn the salt water of the surrounding sea into fresh water. They do this by removing the salt from the water. The island has two desalination plants. One provides the island with 1.5 million gallons (5.7 million L) of fresh water per day, while the second adds another 2.2 million gallons (8.3 million L) to the daily amount.

QUIZ YOURSELF ON St. Croix

1 When did St. Croix become a U.S. territory?

2 From which country did the United States purchase St. Croix?

3 What is the approximate population of St. Croix?

4 What is the name of St. Croix's largest town?

5 Approximately how much rain does St. Croix receive in a year?

6 What is the highest point on St. Croix?

7 Which popular tourist destination tells the story of Danish colonization of the island?

8 How many desalination plants does St. Croix have?

ANSWERS: **1.** 1917 **2.** Denmark **3.** More than 40,000 **4.** Christiansted **5.** 50 inches (127 cm) **6.** Mount Eagle **7.** Christiansted National Historic Site **8.** Two

22 U.S. Virgin Islands

Key Words

ancestry: the family or group of people that someone comes from

archipelago: a group of islands

architecture: a style of building or structure

arid: able to survive in areas with little or no rain

bioluminescent: the ability of some living things to create and emit light

cays: low islands or reefs

colonization: the process of establishing control over foreign lands or peoples

Creole: a person of mixed European and Black ancestry

desalination: the process of removing salt from seawater

dewlaps: folds of loose skin hanging from the neck or throat of an animal

endemic: native and restricted to a certain place

exports: sends goods to another country for sale

geographic: related to the features of Earth's surface in an area

humidity: moisture in the air

Indigenous: relating to a region's original, or native, people

mammals: animals that have hair or fur and feed their young milk

oil refinery: an industrial plant where crude oil is transformed into other products

plantations: farms where cash crops such as cotton and tobacco are grown on a large scale

reptiles: cold-blooded animals that have a backbone and a body that is covered with scales

succulent: a plant with thick leaves and stems that can store a large amount of water

territory: land that is controlled by a particular country or ruler

trade: to buy and sell goods

trade winds: the easterly winds that circle the Earth near the equator

Index

agriculture 9, 16
animals 12, 14, 15, 18, 19
Arawaks 6, 17

Buck Island Reef National Monument 18

Caribs 6
Christiansted 8, 10, 11, 13, 16, 22
Christiansted National Historic Site 16, 22
climate 12, 13
Columbus, Christopher 6, 7
Crucian Christmas Festival 17

Denmark 6, 7, 10, 22

Frederiksted 10, 11, 18, 19

language 8

Mount Eagle 11, 22

oil 9

Protestant Cay 13

Rainbow Beach 19

Salt River Bay National Historical Park and Ecological Preserve 19
St. George Village Botanical Garden 16, 17

Taste of St. Croix 17
tourism 5, 6, 8, 9, 17, 18, 19, 22

water supply 20, 21

St. Croix 23

Get the best of both worlds.

AV2 bridges the gap between print and digital.

The expandable resources toolbar enables quick access to content including **videos**, **audio**, **activities**, **weblinks**, **slideshows**, **quizzes**, and **key words**.

Animated videos make static images come alive.

Resource icons on each page help readers to further **explore key concepts**.

Published by Lightbox Learning Inc.
276 5th Avenue
Suite 704 #917
New York, NY 10001
Website: www.openlightbox.com

Copyright ©2026 Lightbox Learning Inc.
All rights reserved. No part of this publication may be reproduced, stored in a retrieval system, or transmitted in any form or by any means, electronic, mechanical, photocopying, recording, or otherwise, without the prior written permission of the publisher.

Library of Congress Cataloging-in-Publication Data
Names: Wilson, Sierra, author.
Title: St. Croix / Sierra Wilson.
Other titles: Saint Croix
Description: New York, NY : Lightbox Learning Inc., 2026. | Series: U.S. Virgin Islands | Includes index. | Audience: Grades 2-3
Identifiers: LCCN 2024047659 (print) | LCCN 2024047660 (ebook) | ISBN 9798874507428 (library binding) | ISBN 9798874511579 (paperback) | ISBN 9798874507435 (ebook other) | ISBN 9798874507459 (ebook other)
Subjects: LCSH: Saint Croix (United States Virgin Islands)--Juvenile literature.
Classification: LCC F2096 .W56 2026 (print) | LCC F2096 (ebook) | DDC 917.297/22--dc23/eng/20250102
LC record available at https://lccn.loc.gov/2024047659
LC ebook record available at https://lccn.loc.gov/2024047660

Printed in Guangzhou, China
1 2 3 4 5 6 7 8 9 0   29 28 27 26 25

032025
101124

Project Coordinator: Heather Kissock
Designer: Terry Paulhus

Photo Credits
Every reasonable effort has been made to trace ownership and to obtain permission to reprint copyright material. The publisher would be pleased to have any errors or omissions brought to its attention so that they may be corrected in subsequent printings. The publisher acknowledges Getty Images, Alamy, and Shutterstock as its primary image suppliers for this title.